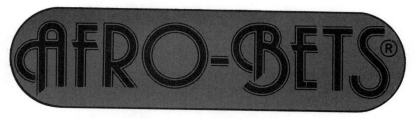

BOOK OF
BLACK
HEROES
From A to Z

AN INTRODUCTION TO
IMPORTANT BLACK ACHIEVERS

FOR YOUNG READERS

written by
WADE HUDSON
VALERIE WILSON WESLEY

designed by
Cheryl Willis Hudson

editorial consultant
P. Mignon Hinds

1988

AFRO-BETS® is a trademark of Cheryl Willis Hudson. The AFRO-BETS® Kids were created by Wade Hudson and Cheryl Willis Hudson. Inquiries should be addressed to Just Us Books, 356 Glenwood Ave., East Orange, NJ 07017. Library of Congress Catalogue Card No. 87-82951. ISBN: 0-940975-46-7 (hardcover), ISBN: 0-940975-02-5 (paperback). Printed in the United States of America.

Hero...one noted for feats of courage or nobility of purpose; especially one who has risked or sacrificed his life. A person prominent in some event, field, period, or cause by reason of special achievements or contributions.

— *The American Heritage Dictionary*

A MESSAGE TO PARENTS

The *AFRO-BETS® Book of Black Heroes from A to Z* was written to introduce young readers to black men and women who are heroes of their time. Some are from the past. Some are contemporary. But they all have overcome great obstacles to make significant contributions.

Black people have made important inventions and discoveries, created great works of art, excelled in science, music, medicine and sports, and have been leaders of great countries. They have played important roles in the history of the world.

All children need to know about these important people. Black children, in particular, need to know about black heroes with whom they can identify. The accomplishments of these black heroes can help children realize that they, too, can overcome obstacles and reach their goals. It is especially important to recognize black heroes who have been omitted from far too many books.

The *AFRO-BETS® Book of Black Heroes from A to Z* is an introduction to just a few important black men and women. We hope that parents and children will find out more about them and share what they have learned.

We could not include in this single book, all the heroes who deserved to be selected. We are, however, already at work on volume two. Other books in this series are planned as well.

We hope you and your child will enjoy reading the *AFRO-BETS® Book of Black Heroes from A to Z*. But more importantly, we hope it will motivate everyone to learn more about the history of black people.

CONTENTS

Page

Aldridge, Ira 1
Ali, Muhammad 2
Anderson, Marian 3
Banneker, Benjamin 4
Bethune, Mary McLeod 5
Cinque, Joseph 6
Coppin, Fanny M. 7
Douglass, Frederick 8
DuBois, William E. B. 9
DuSable, Jean 10
Dunham, Katherine 11
Ellington, Duke 12
Franklin, Aretha 13
Garvey, Marcus 14
Gibson, Althea 15
Hansberry, Lorraine 16
Henson, Matthew 17
Hughes, Langston 18
Hurston, Zora Neale 19
Ingram, Rex 20
Jackson, Jesse 21
Johnson, James Weldon 22
Kay, Ulysses 23
King, Martin Luther, Jr. 24-25
Lewis, Edmonia 26

Locke, Alaine 27
Marshall, Thurgood 28
Mays, Willie 29
Motley, Constance B. 30
Nkrumah, Kwame 31
Owens, Jesse 32
Parks, Rosa 33
Powell, Adam Clayton 34
Quarles, Benjamin 35
Robeson, Paul 36
Rudolph, Wilma 37
Smith, Bessie 38
Still, William Grant 39
Truth, Sojourner 40
Tubman, Harriet 41
Uggams, Leslie 42
Vesey, Denmark 43
Washington, Booker T. 44
Waters, Ethel 45
Wells, Ida B. 46
Wheatley, Phillis 47
X, Malcolm 48
Young, Whitney 49
Zulu, Shaka 50
Suggested Reading 52
Acknowledgments 53-54

THE
BLACK
HEROES

ALDRIDGE, IRA
1805 - 1867
birthplace— New York City

"The Man with the Magical Voice"

When Ira was a boy, very few black children dreamed of becoming actors. Black people who lived in the South were still slaves. Those living in northern cities were free, but they had few opportunities to do what they wanted to do. But Ira was not discouraged. He had a strong, beautiful voice that would someday become famous throughout the world.

When Ira was a young man, he joined a black theater group in New York City. During those times, many white people believed that black people should not be allowed to act in plays. Ira's theater was forced to close. This made Ira very angry. He didn't want to live in a country that would not allow him to develop his talent. He decided to leave the United States and live in Europe.

For the next 40 years, Ira toured England and other parts of Europe. He performed in many plays and was praised and honored by many kings and princes. A portrayal of Othello in Shakespeare's play made him famous. He became one of the best known actors of his day. But he never returned to the United States.

ALI, MUHAMMAD
1942 -
birthplace — Louisville, KY

"The Greatest"

"Float like a butterfly, sting like a bee!" Muhammad Ali's trainer yelled to him. Muhammad hit his opponent with three punches and moved quickly away.

"You got him, champ! You got him!" the trainer yelled again. Muhammad landed another punch that knocked out his rival.

"I'm the greatest!" he declared. "I'm the greatest!" Many people agreed with him.

He was born Cassius Clay, but the bold young fighter changed his name when he joined the Nation of Islam. Muhammad showed his winning style inside and outside the ring. Often he predicted the round in which he would win — and he was right most of the time. He first became heavyweight champion of the world in 1964 when he defeated Sonny Liston.

Muhammad refused to go into the army in 1967 during the Vietnam War. He believed war was wrong. Because of this, his boxing title was taken away from him. He was not allowed to box again for nearly four years. But Muhammad gained the respect of many people for standing up for his beliefs. In 1970, he returned to the ring. He defeated George Foreman in 1974 to regain the heavyweight title. He lost and then won the title again, becoming the first fighter to hold the crown three times. Muhammad retired in 1980.

Muhammad Ali is respected around the world as a champion and humanitarian.

ANDERSON, MARIAN
1902 - 1993
birthplace — Philadelphia, PA

"A Voice Loved Around the World"

Marian Anderson always loved to sing. When she was six, she joined her church choir. Church members were so impressed by her talent, they set up a trust fund to help pay for her musical training.

Marian made her first professional appearance in 1925. She went on to receive worldwide acclaim during her long career as a concert singer.

In spite of her fame, this talented black woman was denied many opportunities. In 1939, the Daughters of the American Revolution refused to let her perform at Constitution Hall in Washington, DC. Eleanor Roosevelt, President Franklin D. Roosevelt's wife and a member of the organization, resigned in protest. She then arranged for Marian to sing on the steps of the Lincoln Memorial. On Easter morning, more than 75,000 people came to hear her concert.

Discrimination did not stop Marian. She was the first black person to sing a leading role at the Metropolitan Opera in New York. She sang in countries all over the world and millions of her records have been sold. Marian Anderson retired in 1965.

3

B

BANNEKER, BENJAMIN
1731 - 1806
birthplace — Endicott, MD

"The Stargazer"

The young man was amazed by the number of stars that appeared in the clear, moonlit sky. "I've never seen so many stars before," he thought. He lay on the ground and began to count them.

This is how Benjamin Banneker spent many of his nights. Neighbors called him "the stargazer."

When Benjamin left school to help on his father's farm, the world became his classroom. He studied the weather, animal life, the stars — everything he could. He read all the books that were available to him. By the time he was 20, Benjamin could answer the most difficult questions in mathematics, science, and philosophy.

In 1761, he carved a wooden clock by hand, using only two models — a pocket watch and an old picture of a clock. It is said that the clock kept nearly perfect time for 50 years.

Benjamin was the first black person to receive a presidential appointment. In 1791, George Washington named him to the commission that laid out the city of Washington, D.C.

Although Benjamin had never been a slave, he spoke out against the system that held his people in bondage. The young man who studied the stars became an astronomer. But he was also a mathematician, inventor, surveyor, philosopher, and abolitionist.

BETHUNE, MARY McLEOD
1875 - 1955
birthplace — Mayesville, SC

"Great Educator"

Mary McLeod Bethune was a determined woman. She helped make education available to thousands of black Americans.

When Mary was a child, many people thought that education was a waste of time for black children. But Mary wanted to go to school, and her parents supported her. She graduated from Moody Bible Institute in 1895 and afterward taught school in Georgia. In 1904, she moved to Daytona, Florida to establish a school for girls.

Mary had only $1.50 in her pocket when she arrived in Daytona. But that didn't stop her. She sold sweet potato pies to raise money for her school. She asked for donations from churches, clubs, and anyone who would help. Her school became Bethune-Cookman University. It is an example of what a determined person can accomplish.

Mary used that same determination to fight for other equal rights for her people. She founded the National Council of Negro Women in 1935. She was also an advisor to four presidents of the United States. Her legacy lives on.

C

CINQUE, JOSEPH
1811 - 1879
birthplace — Sierra Leone,
West Africa

"He Would Not Be a Slave"

Joseph Cinque's arms and legs hurt so much he couldn't move them. He and 52 other young Africans were chained together in the bottom of a ship. They had been kidnapped from their village in Sierra Leone and taken to Havana, Cuba. Now they were on a ship called the *Amistad*. They were being taken to Principe, Cuba, to work as slaves.

Joseph was determined to be free. One night, he and the other Africans escaped from their chains. They went to the deck of the ship, seized weapons, and fought with the ship's crew. All but two crew members were killed.

"You must return us to our home in Africa," Joseph told the two men. But the men still sailed to the United States. The ship was captured off the coast of Connecticut, and Joseph and the others were arrested.

Some people in the United States believed that slavery was wrong. They felt that Joseph should be free. The Supreme Court agreed with them. In 1842, Joseph and the other brave Africans finally were able to return to Africa.

COPPIN, FANNY M.
1836 - 1913
birthplace — Washington, DC

"A Dedicated Educator"

Fanny was born a slave, but an aunt bought her freedom for $125, and then sent her to school in Rhode Island. The thankful young girl never forgot her aunt's generous help. She repaid her by helping others. Fanny became a teacher.

Fanny Coppin was one of the first black women in the United States to receive a college degree. After graduating from Oberlin College in Ohio, she was eager to teach. At first, she taught newly-freed slaves how to read and write. In 1865, she was hired to teach at the Institute for Colored Youth in Philadelphia, Pennsylvania. That school is now called Cheyney University of Pennsylvania. Fanny became principal there in 1869.

Coppin State College, which is located in Baltimore, Maryland, was named in honor of this former slave who became a dedicated educator.

D

DOUGLASS, FREDERICK
1817 - 1895
birthplace — Talbot County, MD

"A Trumpet for Freedom"

As the tall, bearded black man spoke, you could hear a pin drop. When he finished his moving speech, not a dry eye could be found in the entire hall. Many people were troubled to hear about the cruel conditions of slavery. They knew it was bad, but they did not know how often slaves were whipped and killed. Many were surprised to find out that children were taken away from their parents and sold. Frederick Douglass, the greatest anti-slavery speaker of his time, detailed these cruelties and others. Through him, people "experienced" slavery.

Frederick was born a slave in Maryland. He escaped to New York when he was 21 years old. Like many other black people who were able to secure their freedom, he wanted to see his people free, too.

This self-educated man began to speak out against slavery. Frederick became such a well-known leader that he helped convince President Abraham Lincoln to accept black soldiers into the Union Army. His dynamic speeches attracted many followers in America and England.

In 1847, Frederick established the *North Star* newspaper. He was later named a United States marshall in Washington, D.C., and in 1889 he was appointed America's minister to Haiti.

People are still moved today when they read Frederick Douglass's powerful speeches. He was truly "a trumpet for freedom."

DuBOIS,
WILLIAM E. B.
1868 - 1963
birthplace — Great Barrington, MA

"A Gift for Words"

On Tuesday, August 27, 1963, as thousands of people were planning to march on Washington, DC, W.E.B. DuBois died. Some people cried when they heard the news. The great black leader, who had been living in Ghana, West Africa, would be missed.

William was a talented man who was respected throughout the world. He was a scholar, writer, sociologist, philosopher, and leader.

William spent his entire life working for justice and equal rights for black people. He helped organize the National Association for the Advancement of Colored People (NAACP) in 1909. This great civil rights organization has lead the fight for black equality for over 75 years. William worked as editor of *Crisis,* the NAACP magazine. He wrote more than 20 books. *Souls of Black Folks* is the best known.

Many people have been involved in the struggle to make a better America. But no one was more outspoken than William. He supported the fight for black rights in Africa and throughout the world, and he was a leader of the peace movement. Not everyone accepted his ideas. He was attacked by those who disagreed with him. After years of struggle, he moved to Ghana.

On August 28, the historic March on Washington was held. The man with "a gift for words" would have been proud.

DuSABLE, JEAN BAPTISTE
1745 - 1818
birthplace — Haiti

"Founder of Chicago"

Chicago, Illinois, is the third largest city in the United States. But few people know it was founded by a black man, Jean DuSable.

Jean was born in Haiti, the world's oldest black republic. He moved to St. Louis, Missouri, where he became a fur trader. When the British took over St. Louis, Jean moved to Peoria, Illinois where Native Americans helped him establish a successful trading business.

Jean made many trips to Canada to bring back furs. He always passed a place called Eschikagov that he used as a lookout point. In 1774, he built a cabin there for his family. Other pioneers built stores and homes near his post. The settlement grew into a city that became Chicago.

Many years passed before Jean was credited with the founding of Chicago. In 1968, he was finally recognized as the man who founded one of the great cities of the world.

Katherine Dunham performs _L'Ag Ya_, an early creation based on a Martinique fighting dance.

DUNHAM, KATHERINE
1910 -
birthplace — Joliet, IL

"Pioneer of Black Dance"

Katherine Dunham was a dancer, choreographer, and anthropologist. She used her many talents to make an important gift to the world.

When Katherine was a college student, she won a scholarship to study anthropology in Haiti. While she was there, she studied Haitian dances. Katherine was the first person to realize how important these dances were. She believed they could teach people many things about black history and culture. She knew they should be shared with the world.

When Katherine returned to the United States, she brought the dances with her. She formed a company of black dancers that became famous throughout the world. Katherine traveled to many nations and studied the dances of many cultures. She used the beautiful language of dance to teach people about themselves and others. Katherine is known as a pioneer of black dance. Many of the dances she created are still being performed today.

E

ELLINGTON, "Duke"
1899 - 1974
birthplace — Washington, DC

"Take The A Train"

Duke Ellington (born Edward Kennedy Ellington) was a great conductor and composer. His special style of music made him famous around the world. He created jazz songs and orchestra music that influenced many musicians and attracted millions of fans.

As a youngster, Duke showed talent as a pianist. He didn't like to practice, but he did. His friends began to call him "Duke" because he liked to dress in fancy clothes.

Music became Duke's full-time job when he was 18. He became the leader of his own band when he moved to New York City. He soon became a star.

Duke received many awards, and played for kings, queens, and presidents of the United States. He wrote over 1,000 songs and composed music for Broadway shows. He performed in nightclubs as well as concert halls in many countries.

"Take The A Train" and "Sophisticated Lady" are two of Duke Ellington's most popular songs. The world has been made richer by the music created by the "Duke."

FRANKLIN, ARETHA
1942 -
birthplace — Detroit, MI

"Queen of Soul"

R-E-S-P-E-C-T. Respect. That word became very important to black people in the 1960s. Aretha Franklin, the singer who sang about it, earned the respect of everyone who heard her.

Beautiful black voices were always part of Aretha's life. Her father was a well-known preacher. Famous black singers like Dinah Washington, Mahalia Jackson, and B.B. King often visited her home. Music was important to Aretha's family, and it would be a very important part of Aretha's life, too.

When Aretha was 12, she made her first record. By the time she graduated from high school, she knew that she wanted to be a professional singer. At first, she sang only gospel songs. But later she began to sing popular music. Soon, everyone was singing her songs and everyone knew who she was. In 1967, she recorded a number of chart-topping songs. Aretha Franklin became known as the "Queen of Soul." Ever since then, she has been one of the best known singers in the United States.

"Chain of Fools" and "Never Loved a Man" are just two of Aretha's popular songs.

G

GARVEY, MARCUS
1887 - 1940
birthplace — Jamaica,
West Indies

"Back to Africa"

It was one of the most splendid parades ever. Trumpets blasted and drums beat. More than 50,000 people sang proud songs and said proud words. At the head of the parade marched Marcus Garvey in a uniform of purple and gold.

Marcus and the thousands of black people who marched with him were proud of their African heritage. They believed that Africa was a great continent and that Africans were a great people. They were determined to help Africa regain its place in history.

Marcus was born in Jamaica. In 1916, he came to the United States and established the Universal Negro Improvement Association (UNIA), an organization that he had founded in Jamaica. He planned to build black pride in the United States by encouraging black people to build a black nation in Africa. His movement was called the "Back to Africa" movement.

Marcus set up grocery stores, restaurants, and a newspaper. He also established *The Black Star Line,* a fleet of steamships that would return people to their homeland. Thousands of people sent him money. In 1925, the United States government accused Marcus of using the mail to cheat his supporters. He was put in jail, and his ships never sailed.

Although his dream failed, Marcus helped his people develop new feelings of hope and self-respect. He taught black people that they could do great things if they believed in themselves and worked together. That is why many people call him a hero today.

GIBSON, ALTHEA
1927 -
birthplace — Silver, NC

"She Kept Her Eye on the Ball"

Tennis is a very exciting game. But very few black people were recognized as great tennis players before Althea Gibson came along.

Many people believed that tennis wasn't a game black people could play well. But Althea thought differently. She knew anything was possible if she worked very hard.

Althea grew up in New York City. There were very few tennis courts in her neighborhood, but Althea was determined to learn the game and become successful.

She became the first black person to win major titles in tennis. In 1957 and 1958, she won championships at Wimbledon, England and at the U.S. Open in Forest Hills, New York. She also was ranked number one in the world among women players in 1957 and 1958.

Althea Gibson became an international tennis star and an inspiration to others.

H

HANSBERRY, LORRAINE
1930 - 1965
birthplace — Chicago, IL

"Young, Gifted and Black"

I care. I admit it. I care about it all. It takes too much energy <u>not</u> to care!
— from *To Be Young, Gifted and Black*, act II

When Lorraine Hansberry was a girl, her family moved to a white neighborhood. It was during a time when black and white people usually lived in separate parts of town. Many of their neighbors were angry that the Hansberry family had moved into a white section of town. When Lorraine walked to school, many people called her names and made fun of her. She was very frightened.

Lorraine never forgot how hard her family had fought against discrimination. Her famous play, *Raisin in the Sun,* is about a black family that wants to move into a white neighborhood. It is also about the love, pride, and strength that holds many black families together. *Raisin in the Sun* was the first play by a black woman to be produced on Broadway.

Lorraine died at an early age, but many people consider her to be one of America's finest playwrights.

HENSON, MATTHEW
1866 - 1955
birthplace — Charles County, MD

"A Great Explorer"

In March 1907, Matthew Henson and Admiral Robert E. Peary set out to reach the North Pole. They had tried twice before. But the frigid weather and rough terrain stopped them. This time they were determined to reach their goal.

On April 6, the two explorers were only a few miles away from their greatest triumph. Peary was ill, so his black assistant continued. Matthew Henson placed the American flag at the North Pole.

Matthew had always liked adventure. As a teenager, he joined the crew of a ship bound for China as a cabin boy. He also sailed to Europe, Africa, and the South Pacific.

Matthew was 21 when he met Admiral Peary. They made many trips together. During the Admiral's expeditions to the North Pole, Matthew played an important role. He spoke the language of the Eskimos, built sleds, and trained teams of dogs. He solved many problems and gave valuable advice.

Nearly 81 years went by before the accomplishments of this great explorer were fully recognized. On April 6, 1988, Matthew's remains were reburied with full military honors at Arlington National Cemetery in Washington, DC. His great feat had finally been acknowledged.

HUGHES, LANGSTON
1902 - 1967
birthplace — Joplin, MO

"A Pen for a Sword"

I've known rivers:
I've known rivers ancient as the world and older than the
   flow of human blood in human veins,
My soul has grown deep like rivers.

— from "The Negro Speaks of Rivers"

No one enjoyed writing more than Langston Hughes. He was a poet, but he also wrote plays, songs, and books.

Langston wrote about the lives and conditions of black Americans. People enjoyed his warm and humorous style. He had a gift for making others understand how black people lived, worked, talked, and played.

Langston's first poem was published when he was 19. "The Negro Speaks of Rivers" is still one of his most popular poems.

The Harlem Renaissance in the 1920s and 1930s was an important era for black writers and artists. Langston was one of the most important writers of that period.

He continued to write and travel until his death in 1967. Langston published ten volumes of poetry and numerous short stories and anthologies. He also produced plays and operas. He was recognized throughout the world as one of America's finest writers.

In 1960, the NAACP presented Langston with the Spingarn Medal, declaring him "Poet Laureate of the Negro Race."

HURSTON, ZORA NEALE
1903 - 1960
birthplace — Eatonville, FL

"A Southern Genius"

Here is peace. She pulled in her horizon like a giant fish-net. Pulled it around the waist of the world and draped it over her shoulder. So much of life in its meshes. She called in her soul to come and see!

— from *Their Eyes Were Watching God*

Zora was a bright little girl with a mischievous spirit. Her father warned that her curiosity would get her in trouble — that "the white folks wouldn't stand for it." But her mother told her to "jump at the sun," and that is just what Zora did.

Zora was born in Eatonville, a self-governing black town in Florida. She loved to listen to stories on the back porch of the general store where people in her town gathered. It was there that Zora developed a love for language and folktales.

Zora was a writer, but she also studied and collected folktales. She celebrated the lives of black people in her novels and folktale collections. She followed her mother's advice. Zora was never afraid to express her feelings or live the way she wanted to live. Writers admire her unique gift of telling stories in the wonderful style that captures everyday life. One of her most popular novels is *Their Eyes Were Watching God*.

INGRAM, REX
1895 - 1969
birthplace — riverboat on
the Mississippi

"A Dynamic Actor"

Rex Ingram was one of America's most talented actors. He appeared in movies and stage productions that were enjoyed by Americans everywhere.

Rex was born aboard a riverboat on which his father worked. He became interested in acting when he attended military school. In 1919, he began his acting career in movies with a role in the first Tarzan movie. Afterwards, he was featured in such films as *Lord Jim*, *Beau Geste*, *King Kong*, *Green Pastures*, and *Huckleberry Finn*.

Although Rex was an excellent actor, he was denied many roles because of his color. But he loved to act and didn't get discouraged.

Rex was one of the few black actors to serve on the board of directors of the Studio Actors Guild, the actors' union.

One of Rex's best known roles was in *Cabin in the Sky* in which he played Lucifer, Jr. This famous movie, released in 1943, had an all-black cast that featured some of the finest performers of that time.

JACKSON, JESSE
1941 -
birthplace — Greenville, SC

"The Country Preacher"

"Ladies and gentlemen," said the announcer. "I would like to introduce the man who will be the 1984 Democratic nominee for President of the United States — Reverend Jesse Jackson!"

Everyone clapped and cheered. Jesse proudly stepped to the front of the platform. He raised his arms and gave the "V" sign for victory. History was being made.

In 1984, Jesse Jackson became the first black man to run for president. Few people in Jesse's hometown could have imagined how important he would become.

When he was young, many children teased him because his mother wasn't married when he was born. But Jesse always knew he was a special person. He was determined to succeed. In high school, he became an outstanding football player and school leader.

During the 1960s, Jesse joined the civil rights movement. He became a member of the Southern Christian Leadership Conference (SCLC), and worked closely with Dr. Martin Luther King, Jr. In 1967, he gained wide power and respect when he was appointed director of "Operation Breadbasket," a program that helped people in large cities obtain jobs and housing. A year later, Jesse became a minister.

In 1971, he organized Operation PUSH (People United to Save Humanity). This organization is still fighting for equality for all.

In 1988, Jesse ran an even stronger campaign to gain the Democratic nomination for president. He won a number of states and finished second in many others. Some people were surprised by the support he received. Although he did not win, Jesse Jackson has risen from a humble beginning to become one of the most powerful men in America.

JOHNSON, JAMES WELDON
1871 - 1938
birthplace — Jacksonville, FL

"A Way with Words"

Lift every voice and sing,
'til earth and heaven ring —
Ring with the harmonies of liberty

These were beautiful words that would be sung long after James Weldon Johnson was dead. In 1900, James wrote this verse to music composed by his brother, John. Their song "Lift Every Voice and Sing" became known as the Negro National Anthem. Generations of black people have sung their song with pride.

James was an educator, poet, novelist, diplomat, and civil rights leader. He cared deeply about his people and worked to improve their lives. In 1920, he became the executive secretary of the NAACP.

Black culture was important to James. He wrote many important books about black people's contributions to music, religion, and theater. He also wrote a novel called *The Autobiography of an Ex-Colored Man.* James also served as a diplomat and consul for the United States in Venezuela and Nicaragua.

KAY, ULYSSES
1917 -
birthplace — Tucson, AZ

"A Classical Giant"

Some people believed that classical music was too difficult for black people to master. Men like William Grant Still, Dean Dixon, and Ulysses Kay proved them wrong. These talented black men became outstanding composers and conductors.

Ulysses Kay decided to make music his career when he was young. He had always loved music, but he knew he had to study hard if he wanted to succeed. He attended the Eastman School of Music, the Berkshire Music Center, and Yale University. He learned to compose.

After serving in the United States Navy during World War II, Ulysses quickly became the most important black composer of classical music in the United States. He received numerous awards, including the Gershwin Memorial Prize, a Broadcast Music, Inc. award, and an American Broadcasting Company prize.

"Oboe Concerto" (1940), "A Short Overture" (1947), and "The Juggler of Our Lady" (1962) are three of his most popular works.

Ulysses Kay will be remembered not only as a great composer, but also as a black pioneer in classical music.

KING, MARTIN LUTHER, JR.
1929 - 1968
birthplace — Atlanta, GA

"Drum Major for Justice"

It was 1955. A group of black people gathered in a local church in Montgomery, Alabama. Many were angry because Rosa Parks had been arrested for refusing to give her bus seat to a white man. They wanted to do something about the discrimination they had faced in Montgomery. A young minister was chosen as their leader. His name was Martin Luther King, Jr.

Martin was the son of a minister. So, many people assumed he would become a minister, too.

Young Martin was an excellent student. He studied hard, but he enjoyed it because he loved to learn. In 1948, Martin graduated from Morehouse College. He was only 19. Three years later, he received a bachelor of divinity degree from Crozer Theological Seminary. Boston University awarded him a doctorate degree in 1955.

Martin was 25 when he was chosen to become pastor of the Dexter Avenue Baptist Church in Montgomery. He quickly impressed church members with his speaking and organizing abilities. His stirring sermons drew people from all over the city. Many of the people assembled knew this was the man to lead them.

The bus boycott that Martin led ended segregated seating on Montgomery public buses. But he did not stop there. Martin headed a long struggle for equal justice in America. He helped win many rights that all Americans now enjoy. Just 30 years ago, in many American cities, black people could not vote. They could not drink from the same water fountain or use the same rest room as white people. Black children could not go to the same schools that white children attended. Martin helped to end these injustices.

It wasn't easy. Thousands of people went to jail. Many were beaten and killed. But Martin didn't believe in violence. He used peaceful methods of protest, such as sit-ins, marches, and boycotts.

In 1963, he led the historic March on Washington, where he gave his famous "I Have a Dream" speech. A year later he was awarded the Nobel Peace Prize. And, in 1986, a national holiday was declared to honor this great American. The people assembled in 1955 couldn't have known how great Martin would become.

Dr. Martin Luther King, Jr. was assassinated in Memphis, Tennessee on April 4, 1968 by James Earl Ray. He was only 39 years old, but he did as much as anyone could to secure equality and justice for all Americans.

L

LEWIS, EDMONIA
1845 - 1890
birthplace — Albany, NY

"She Made Stone 'Talk'"

Edmonia Lewis was such a talented sculptor she seemed to make stones "talk." Her sculptures tell a story. One of her most famous, *Forever Free,* is a study of a freedman greeting freedom. One of his hands is clenched in a fist, the other protects his wife. Many people believe that this sculpture captures the two strong feelings that many black people felt when they were declared free — joy in their freedom and fear that it would be taken away.

Edmonia also created busts of famous people who fought to end slavery. Her busts of John Brown, Charles Sumner, and William Story truly captured the spirit and determination that made these men strong fighters for justice.

Edmonia's father was a black American and her mother was a Native American. She was one of the first women to attend Oberlin College. After leaving Oberlin, Edmonia moved to Boston and further developed her artistic talent. Later she went to Rome, Italy, where she set up a studio.

Edmonia was also a fighter for freedom. She was involved in the "Underground Railroad" that made it possible for slaves to escape to the North. She also helped organize one of the first black regiments to fight in the Civil War. Edmonia was one of the first black Americans to be recognized as a great artist.

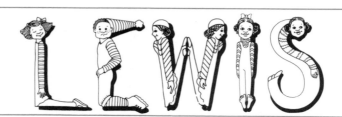

LOCKE, ALAINE
1886 - 1954
birthplace — Philadelphia, PA

"A Black Scholar"

It must be increasingly recognized that the Negro has already made very substantial contributions, not only in his folk-art and music especially, which has already found appreciation, but in larger, though humbler and less acknowledged ways.

— from *The New Negro*

Alaine enjoyed helping people. It made him feel good to help others succeed. He especially liked to help those who were creative. Many aspiring writers and artists looked to him for encouragement and assistance.

Alaine was an educator, writer, historian, and critic. He wrote many books and articles that helped people understand the contributions made by black Americans to American culture.

In 1907, he became the first black person selected as a Rhodes Scholar. The Rhodes Scholarship is awarded to only a few outstanding students each year.

Alaine was one of the leaders of the Harlem Renaissance during the 1920s and 1930s. At first, people recognized only black writers. Alaine helped make them aware of black artists and musicians, too.

For 36 years he taught at Howard University. Alaine was one of America's brightest scholars.

M

MARSHALL, THURGOOD
1908 - 1993
birthplace — Baltimore, MD

"Supreme Court Justice"

Thurgood Marshall always cared about his fellow man. When he practiced law in Baltimore, Maryland, he represented many clients without getting paid.

Thurgood graduated with honors from Howard University Law School. In 1940, he was named chief counsel for the National Association for the Advancement of Colored People. During his years with the NAACP, Thurgood and his staff won 29 out of 32 Supreme Court cases. His most famous victory came in the 1954 *Brown* vs. *Board of Education of Topeka, Kansas* case. This historic decision overturned the "separate but equal" doctrine that had justified segregation since 1896.

In 1965, Thurgood was appointed solicitor general of the United States. When a vacancy occurred on the Supreme Court, President Lyndon Johnson nominated him for the seat. In 1967, this great jurist became the first black justice of the United States Supreme Court. Thurgood Marshall dedicated his life to protecting the rights of all Americans.

MAYS, WILLIE
1931 -
birthplace — Westfield, AL

"Say, Hey"

Willie ran fast. He hit like a champ. He slugged 660 home runs. For over 20 years, this great player proved he could do it all. He was one of the most exciting men to ever play professional baseball.

Willie started his career in the Negro Leagues. At that time, black players were not allowed to play with white players in major league baseball. So they formed their own leagues.

The New York Giants bought Willie's contract from the Birmingham Black Barons in 1950. The Giants sent him to a minor league team to gain more experience. But Willie played so well, the Giants invited him to join their team. He became a popular star.

Willie usually greeted people by saying "Say, Hey." He became known as the "Say, Hey Kid." After a long, successful career with the Giants and the New York Mets, Willie was elected to the Baseball Hall of Fame in 1979.

MOTLEY, CONSTANCE BAKER

1921 -

birthplace — New Haven, CT

"Woman of Distinction"

Constance was born in the small state of Connecticut. But the legal battles she won made a big difference in the lives of her people.

As a lawyer, Constance fought many important civil rights battles. One of her most famous victories gave James Meredith the right to become a student at the University of Mississippi. During the 1950s, it was against the law for black and white students in the South to attend college together. Constance fought for James Meredith's right to attend the school of his choice. Her victory struck an important blow against segregation in southern universities.

In 1965, Constance was elected Manhattan borough president in New York City. She was the first black person *and* first woman to hold that powerful office. In 1966, President Lyndon Johnson appointed her a United States district judge. Constance Baker Motley has proven that the courts and law are powerful weapons in the fight for justice.

NKRUMAH, KWAME
1909 - 1972
birthplace — Ghana,
West Africa

"Africa Must Unite"

The African continent once had many strong and powerful nations. But in the 15th century, Dutch, French, and other Europeans took over many African countries. For over 400 years, Africans were forced to live under foreign rule. Throughout Africa, people were denied rights as citizens in their own land.

Kwame Nkrumah spent most of his life fighting to bring independence to his country. Born in the western province of the Gold Coast, Kwame was educated in the United States and England. He was active in organizations that fought for reform in his country. He became prime minister in 1952. In 1957 the Gold Coast became the first black nation in Africa to regain its independence. Ghana was chosen as its official name. Kwame Nkrumah became president in 1960.

Other African nations looked to Nkrumah for guidance in their struggle for independence. They knew he believed "Africa must unite."

OWENS, JESSE
1913 - 1980
birthplace — Danville, AL

"A Blaze of Glory"

The 1936 Olympic games that were held in Nazi Germany were about more than just sports. Adolph Hitler, the Nazi leader, said that Germans were a "master race." Many Germans believed him. They thought that Germany should rule the world. Hitler and his followers were sure that the Olympic games would prove they were right. But Jesse Owens had other ideas.

Jesse came from a poor, black family. He worked very hard in school and won a scholarship to Ohio State University. In college, he became a track star.

In 1936, Jesse showed the world that he was a great athlete. In a blaze of glory, he won three gold medals — in the broad jump, the 100-meter dash, and the 200-meter dash — and his speed helped his team win a gold medal in the 440-meter relay. Jesse changed history by setting new world records.

Adolph Hitler was furious. A black man had embarrassed him before the world. Jesse proved that people are winners because of their talent, not because of their color or nationality.

PARKS, ROSA
1913 -
birthplace — Tuskegee, AL

"Mother of the Movement"

Rosa's feet ached as she walked to the Cleveland Avenue bus stop. It was 1955 in Montgomery, Alabama. People were rushing home after a hard day of work.

When the bus arrived, all seats were quickly taken. Some people had to stand. Black people could only sit in the back of the bus. The front section was reserved for whites. Although Rosa sat in the section reserved for black people, the bus driver ordered her and three other black people to give their seats to white people. Rosa refused and she was arrested.

Rosa's refusal to give up her seat helped to start a movement against segregation. The leader of that movement was a young minister named Dr. Martin Luther King, Jr. Her actions that afternoon in Montgomery guaranteed her place in history.

Rosa Parks often worked two jobs to help support her family. She always found time, however, to help make Montgomery a better city for her people. She was an active member of the local NAACP.

Rosa Parks still fights to make America a better land. She is an administrative assistant to U. S. Representative John Conyers in Detroit, Michigan.

33

POWELL, ADAM CLAYTON, JR.
1908 - 1972
birthplace — New Haven, CT

"Keep the Faith"

Adam was a child when he first learned the power of words. It was a lesson he never forgot. His father, Adam Clayton Powell, Sr., was an important minister in Harlem, the largest black community in the United States. He often spoke about the injustices that many black Americans faced.

When Adam grew up, he decided to become a minister like his father had been. He was chosen to become pastor of his father's church, the Abyssinian Baptist Church.

Adam knew that the injustices he fought against in New York City could be found elsewhere in America. So he decided to run for Congress and fight for justice for all Americans. He won his first election in 1944.

Adam accomplished many things in Congress. He helped to raise the minimum wage and was one of the strongest supporters of education. He fought to keep the government from spending money for projects that discriminated against black people. Adam became chairman of the very important House Committee on Education and Labor in 1961.

In 1967, Adam was accused of misusing public funds. He was stripped of his seat in Congress. But the man who had urged black Americans to "keep the faith" did not give up. The people of Harlem elected him again in 1969, and public pressure helped him get back his seat.

QUARLES, BENJAMIN
1904 -
birthplace — Boston, MA

"Great Historian"

To prove that he was not a slave, a free Negro had to carry around with him a certificate of freedom. Numbered, registered, and issued by the courts, these "free papers" gave the name, stature, and complexion of the Negro and indicated how his freedom had been obtained. Free papers had to be renewed periodically, for which a fee was assessed.

— from *The Negro in the Making of America*

When Benjamin was growing up in Boston, Massachusetts, there were few books about black history. So when he became a man, he decided to write books that told about the many important contributions that black people had made to American society.

In his research, Benjamin found that black people had played important roles in American history. He also found that most books did not include their achievements. He knew it was up to him to fill in the missing facts. Benjamin wrote about how black people fought for victory in the Revolutionary and the Civil Wars. He also wrote about Frederick Douglass and Abraham Lincoln.

The historical research done by Benjamin and other black historians has helped all Americans appreciate black contributions. Benjamin received many awards for his achievements. He was a professor at Morgan State University in Baltimore, Maryland until he retired.

R

ROBESON, PAUL
1898 - 1976
birthplace — Princeton, NJ

"A Man for All Seasons"

As Paul Robeson walked to the stage, the audience rose to its feet with applause. It was their way of saying, "Welcome home, we love you." The year was 1963. Paul had recently returned to the United States after living in Europe for five years. These people had come to show how much they appreciated him.

Paul was a singer, actor, scholar, lawyer, humanitarian, and athlete. He spoke several languages. There weren't many things he couldn't do.

He graduated from Rutgers University with honors and was selected as an All-American football player. His acting career began in 1921 at the Harlem YMCA. A year later, his talent was recognized in the play *Emperor Jones.* In a few years, Paul was known around the world as a great singer and actor. His rich baritone voice brought joy to millions.

Because of his fame, Paul knew many people would listen to him. So he spoke out against the racism and injustice he saw in America and the world. Some people tried to silence him. In 1950, the United States Government took away his passport. He couldn't perform in other countries, and concert halls in America were closed to him. He was unable to earn a living doing what he loved most. But Paul still spoke out. When the government was forced to give back his passport in 1958, he went to England. He didn't return until 1963.

Despite the many attempts to discredit him, people around the world continued to love and respect Paul Robeson.

He will always be remembered as a person who made great sacrifices to help his fellow man.

RUDOLPH, WILMA
1940 -
birthplace — Clarksville, TN

"A Golden Track Star"

Wilma never liked to lose. She always tried very hard to be a winner — and her determined spirit usually led to success.

When Wilma was a child she had to wear a brace on her left leg. She had been crippled by polio, but she was determined to walk without her brace. Soon she learned to walk *and* run without it.

In high school, Wilma won many races. She was also a star basketball player. In 1956, she scored 803 points during one season. Tennessee State University gave her a scholarship so she could run on their track team.

While competing in the 1960 Olympic games held in Rome, Wilma became the first woman to win three Olympic medals in track. She was recognized as the world's fastest woman runner. In 1960, the Associated Press voted her female athlete of the year.

Wilma Rudolph's winning spirit still inspires athletes today.

S

SMITH, BESSIE
1894 - 1937
birthplace — Chattanooga, TN

"Empress of the Blues"

When Bessie was young, Ma Rainey, the first of the great blues singers, took her under her wing and helped her find a job. Blues is very special music, and not everyone can sing it well. Ma Rainey knew a good blues singer when she heard one. She was sure that the young singer would become great.

Bessie sang about things in life that give people "the blues" — poverty, racism, and love that is not returned. Her strong, beautiful voice was so powerful, she didn't need a microphone. Her songs captured the sadness and joy of many black Americans.

Bessie sang in many clubs and small southern theaters. In 1923, she went to New York to make her first record. Many recordings followed. "Down Hearted Blues" sold more than two million copies.

Many people who heard Bessie sing believed that "the Empress" was one of the greatest blues singers who ever lived.

STILL, WILLIAM GRANT
1895 - 1978
birthplace — Woodville, MS

"The Dean of Black Composers"

William loved music. He could create songs, but he wanted others to be able to play and enjoy them. He knew he must learn how to write down his music.

For many years, some people thought that black musicians could not play "serious" music. They believed that music by black composers was not important enough to write down. William knew they were wrong.

He attended the Oberlin Conservatory of Music and the New England Conservatory of Music. He studied very hard and learned how to compose. He created symphonies, operas, ballet music, and musical poems. William successfully combined black and European musical traditions. His beautiful compositions were enjoyed by many people.

William was determined to show that black conductors could lead orchestras as well as white conductors. In 1936, he became the first black person to conduct a major orchestra in the United States. He led the Los Angeles Philharmonic Orchestra in a performance of one of his own compositions.

TRUTH, SOJOURNER
1797 - 1883
birthplace — Hurley, NY

"Freedom's Messenger"

Sojourner was born a slave and was named Isabella Baumfree. New York, the state where she lived, outlawed slavery in 1827. But Sojourner's master didn't care. He would not free her. So she ran away.

When Sojourner was 46 years old, she decided to start her own campaign against slavery. She could not stand to see her people suffer any longer. She changed her name to Sojourner Truth. She chose that name because she planned to travel from place to place to tell the truth about slavery.

Sojourner carried her anti-slavery message throughout the North. She spoke to anyone who would listen — and to those who wouldn't, too. She was a great speaker. Some people compared her to Frederick Douglass.

Sojourner was often beaten for speaking out against slavery. But this brave woman could not be stopped. She had a mission.

In 1863, Abraham Lincoln signed the Emancipation Proclamation that outlawed slavery. But the southern states did not recognize the law until they were defeated. After the Civil War, Sojourner fought for black equality and women's rights. She dedicated her life to opening the doors of freedom for all people.

TUBMAN, HARRIET
c. 1820 - 1913
birthplace — Dorcester County, MD

"Black Moses"

The small band of runaway slaves hid behind trees. They huddled together to hide from the cruel slave catchers. Would the runaways be caught and taken back to slavery? Or would they escape to freedom in the North?

"Not a sound from anyone!" a voice warned. It was Harriet Tubman. She knew the risks and dangers they all faced. This trip to lead slaves from the South was not her first.

Soon the slave catchers were gone. The group of runaway slaves traveled through the dark woods and escaped to the North. "Black Moses" had struck again.

Harriet Tubman led more than 300 slaves to freedom. Although Harriet had escaped from slavery, she made many dangerous trips back to help others find the road to freedom. She used an established route called the "Underground Railroad." Along this route, friends and supporters provided safe hiding places, food, and clothing for the runaway slaves.

Angry slave masters offered huge rewards for Harriet's capture, but she managed to fool them again and again. As a "conductor" on the "Underground Railroad," Harriet Tubman never lost a passenger.

U

UGGAMS, LESLIE
1943 -
birthplace — New York, NY

"A Young Star"

Leslie sang almost from the time she could talk. When she was six years old, Leslie made her singing debut. A short while later she appeared in the television series "Beulah," starring Ethel Waters.

In 1961, Leslie became a cast member on the popular program "Sing Along With Mitch." In a short time, her charming voice and perky style attracted fans everywhere. She was a star at only 18 years old. For several years, she was the only black entertainer to be seen regularly on television.

Leslie's parents were also entertainers. Her father was a singer, and her mother had performed as a chorus girl at Harlem's famous Cotton Club.

Leslie is not only a singer, but also an actress. She starred in the award-winning television movie "Roots" which was based upon the book of the same name. This story details the history of a black family from its beginning in Africa to present-day America. She is still performing today.

Slaves plan a revolt.

V

VESEY, DENMARK
1767 - 1822
birthplace — Haiti

"Lover of Freedom"

Denmark Vesey stared out at the angry crowd of whites who were waiting to see him hanged. But he was not afraid. It didn't matter what they thought. He was willing to die for freedom.

It was summer in Charleston, South Carolina, the city where Denmark lived. Slavery was an important part of life in America. Although Denmark had bought his freedom with money he won in a lottery, he could not buy his children's freedom.

Denmark became a dedicated fighter against slavery. He believed black people were being held illegally. To free slaves in the Charleston area, he planned an uprising. He recruited allies and drew up a battle plan. He planned to take over the city on the second Sunday in July of 1822. But his plan was discovered. Denmark and some of his followers were arrested and sentenced to be hanged. Although he did not succeed, Denmark's efforts focused attention on the struggle to end slavery.

It was quiet now. The crowd moved away. The man who just wanted to see his people free was dead. It seemed strange that two days later, on July 4th, the country celebrated its own freedom.

W

WASHINGTON, BOOKER T.
1856 - 1915
birthplace — Franklin County, VA

"A Great Leader"

Booker was a small boy when slavery ended. He worked in the salt mines of West Virginia from four in the morning until late at night to earn enough money for food. Booker was convinced that education was the key to success. He was determined to learn. He studied by the light of the fire each night after he came home from work.

When he was 15, Booker left home and entered Hampton Institute. He cleaned buildings and classrooms to pay his college tuition. He wanted to become a teacher. But more important things lay ahead.

In 1881, Booker T. Washington was chosen to head a newly established school for black students called Tuskegee Normal and Industrial Institute. There were two small, wooden buildings and 30 students when he arrived. Under his leadership, Tuskegee grew and became an important school for black students.

Booker became a leader of his people, too. He believed that black Americans should learn trades to build up their economic position. He felt this should be done, even before fighting for integration and equality. Some people disagreed with him, especially William E.B. DuBois. But Booker continued to fight in his own way for equality.

Booker T. Washington was born in a slave cabin. But he became one of the most powerful black Americans of his time.

WATERS, ETHEL
1896 - 1977
birthplace — Chester, PA

"An Actress with a Golden Voice"

When Ethel was a little girl, her family was so poor she had to steal food to eat. When she was 13, she worked as a maid for less than five dollars a day. But Ethel never lost hope. She was sure that someday her life would change. She knew that she was talented and she believed in herself.

Ethel had a beautiful voice. She could sing jazz songs and the blues. Her singing style made ordinary songs sound very special. Many people came to hear her sing, and she became famous. But she wanted to do more.

She began to act in plays and movies. People who thought she was a great singer now knew that she was a great actress, too. Ethel's beautiful voice and dramatic talent established her as one of the most important actresses of her time.

In 1950, she won the New York Drama Critics Award for her performance in the Broadway play *A Member of the Wedding*.

WELLS, IDA B.
1869 - 1931
birthplace — Holly Springs, MS

"A Warrior with Words"

Ida B. Wells' parents were strong people who were born slaves. By their example, they taught Ida courage and strength. They also taught her to love freedom as much as they did. When she was 14, her parents died of yellow fever. After their death, Ida worked as a teacher and raised her seven brothers and sisters by herself. She never forgot her parents' lessons.

During the 19th century, black people suffered many injustices. Many black families had their land stolen. Many black people were murdered. Many black men were hanged for crimes they didn't commit. Ida was very angry about these cruelties and decided to do something about them. She knew that words could be strong weapons, so she fought with words.

Ida wrote about the many injustices she saw. She made people aware of how black people were suffering. In 1894, she published *The Red Record,* the first book to document the lynching of black Americans. She was also a founder of the NAACP. Ida became known in the United States and throughout the world as a fighter for justice.

WHEATLEY, PHILLIS
1753 - 1784
birthplace — Senegal, West Africa

"A Poet for Her Times"

The goddess comes, she moves divinely fair
Olive and Laurel binds her golden hair;
wherever shines this native of the skies
unnumbered charms and recent graces rise.

— From "To His Excellency, General Washington"

Phillis was very young when she was stolen from her parents and brought to America. She would never forget her parents, her African homeland, or her trip on the horrible slave ship. She was bought by the Wheatleys, a family of white merchants. As their slave, she had to do whatever they asked.

But the Wheatleys soon realized that Phillis was a very special child. They taught her how to read and write. By the time she was 14, she had written her first poem.

Soon many people began to read her poetry. One of her poems, which was dedicated to George Washington, brought her much attention. In 1773, Phillis published a collection of poems entitled *Poems on Various Subjects, Religious and Moral*.

Phillis Wheatley was only 31 years old when she died. But she will be remembered as one of America's first black poets.

X

X, MALCOLM
1925 - 1965
birthplace — Omaha, NB

"Fighter for Freedom"

No one expressed the anger that many black Americans felt during the 1950s and 1960s more vividly than Malcolm X. He lashed out at society's unfair treatment of his people and warned America that black people would no longer accept racial injustice.

Born Malcolm Little, he was only six years old when his father was killed. His mother had a nervous breakdown several years later and Malcolm was sent to live in a foster home.

Malcolm had trouble adjusting to life without his family. Although he was a good student, he dropped out of school at 15. Before he was 21, he was sent to prison for burglary.

In prison, Malcolm discovered a religious group called the Nation of Islam. This organization of Black Muslims helped him find a new purpose in life. Malcolm Little became Malcolm X, the leading spokesman for the Nation of Islam. He established its national newspaper and helped to organize bakeries and stores. Many black Americans looked to Malcolm as their leader.

Malcolm left the Nation of Islam in 1963 and formed the Organization of Afro-American Unity. Following a trip to Mecca, he changed his name to El Hajj Malik al-Shabazz. His fight for freedom continued.

On February 21, 1965, Malcolm was killed by assassins. But he had already made his mark in the struggle for justice for black Americans.

YOUNG, WHITNEY M., JR.
1921 - 1971
birthplace —Lincoln Ridge, KY

"A Dynamic Leader"

It has become necessary for me to face realistically the true state of America's development as it seeks to make operational, and give honest meaning to, its creed of equal opportunity and justice for all.

— from *To Be Equal*

The 1960s were a time of change. Many black people fought for civil rights and equality. Whitney Young, Jr., was a strong leader who worked hard to make a better life for his people.

At first, Whitney wanted to become a doctor. But he saw many problems in the world that bothered him. He decided that he could do more to help people by becoming a social worker. Eventually he became the dean of Atlanta University's School of Social Work. In 1961, Whitney was appointed head of the National Urban League. He knew that there were many rich people in the United States who could give help to poor people. He worked to find ways for them to contribute.

Whitney convinced many corporations and foundations to sponsor self-help programs that would help guide black people toward jobs, education, and housing. Through his leadership, many people were given the help they needed to build themselves a better life.

Z

ZULU, SHAKA
1787 - 1828
birthplace — South Africa

"A Great General"

The mere mention of Shaka's name made his enemies tremble with fear. He was one of the greatest African generals who ever lived. His army was one of the most fearless in the world.

Shaka was born a Zulu prince, but his father would not claim him as his son. He and his mother Nandi wandered from village to village tryng to find a home. People called Shaka's mother names, and children threw stones at him. But these hard times made Shaka strong. He had been told that he was destined to rule the Zulus and he never forgot it.

The Mtetwa, powerful rivals of the Zulus, accepted Shaka and his mother into their clan. Shaka became a great warrior. In the early 1800s, the king of the Mtetwa ordered Shaka to conquer the Zulus. Shaka was pleased. Now was his chance to claim his birthright. He conquered the Zulus and became their leader.

Shaka organized his army into a powerful force that conquered many other clans. He used new military techniques and weapons. Under his leadership, the Zulus became the most powerful nation in southern Africa. Shaka remains a hero to the Zulu nation today.

SUGGESTED READING LIST

Readers may find further information about black heroes in the following books:

Bennett, Lerone, Jr., *Pioneers in Protest*, Johnson Publishing Co., Chicago. (Teens and Up)

Boone-Jones, Margaret, *Martin Luther King, Jr.*, Childrens Press, Chicago. (Ages 8-12)

Chaplik, Dorothy, *Up With Hope, A Biography of Jesse Jackson*, Dillon Press, Inc., Minneapolis, MN. (Young Teens)

Clark, Margaret C., *Benjamin Banneker, Astronomer and Scientist*, Garrard Publishing Co., Champaign, IL. (Ages 8-12)

Collier, Lincoln, and Collier, Christopher, *Jump Ship to Freedom*, Dell Yearling Paperback, New York. (Ages 5-11)

Greenfield, Eloise, *Mary McLeod Bethune*, Thomas Y. Crowell, New York. (Young Teens)

Haber, Louis, *Black Pioneers of Science and Invention*, Harcourt, New York. (Ages 4-8)

Hamilton, Virginia, *W.E.B. DuBois, A Biography*, Thomas Y. Crowell, New York. (Young Teens)

Lester, Julius, *To Be a Slave*, Scholastic Books, New York. (Ages 8-11)

Lipsyte, Robert, *Free To Be Muhammad Ali*, Harper & Row, New York, New York. (Young Teens)

Lowery, Linda, *Martin Luther King Day*, Carolrhoda Books, Minneapolis, MN. (Ages 4-8)

McGovern, Ann, *Wanted Dead or Alive: The Story Of Harriet Tubman*, Scholastic Books, New York. (Ages 8-11)

Patterson, Lillie, *Frederick Douglass: Freedom Fighter*, Garrard Publishing Co., Champaign, IL. (Ages 4-8)

Patterson, Lillie, *Martin Luther King, Jr., Man of Peace*, Garrard Publishing Co., Champaign, IL. (Ages 8-12)

Santrey, Laurence, *Young Frederick Douglass: Fight For Freedom*, Troll Associates. (Young Readers)

Stein, Conrad R., *The Story of the Montgomery Bus Boycott*, Childrens Press, Chicago. (Ages 4-8)

Stein, Conrad R., *The Story of The Underground Railroad*, Childrens Press, Chicago. (Ages 4-8)

Strickland, Dorothy S., *Listen Children*, Bantam, New York. (All Ages)

ACKNOWLEDGMENTS

We would like to thank the following people for their valuable assistance in preparing this book: Mitchell and Jewel Black, Printing Delite; Vera Toson and James Rabkin, Verdon Graphics; Culverson Blair; Wendy Lewison; Carol Drisko; Betty Odabashian, Schomburg Center for Research in Black Culture, New York Public Library; Linda F. McClure, Morgan State University.

PHOTO CREDITS

Arista Records, 13
Bettmann Newsphotos: 2, 15, 16, 20, 21, 24, 25, 28, 29, 32, 38, 42, cover
Courtesy John Butler, 50
Boston Athenaeum, 26
Katherine Dunham Museum, East St. Louis, IL, 11
The Dusable Museum of African American History, Inc., Chicago, IL, 10
Ghanian Embassy, 31
The Granger Collection, 3
Historical Pictures Services, Chicago, IL, 43
Morgan State University, Office of The President
National Portrait Gallery, Smithsonian Institute DC: 1, 6, 8, 27, 40, 44, 47, cover
Schomburg Center for Research in Black Culture, The New York Public Library
Astor, Lenox and Tilden Foundations: 4, 5, 9, 12, 14, 17, 18, 19, 22, 23, 30, 33, 34, 36, 37, 39, 41, 45, 46, 48, 49, cover

PERMISSIONS

p. vii Copyright © 1981 by Houghton Mifflin Company. Adapted and reprinted by permission from The American Heritage Dictionary of the English Language.

p. 16 from **To Be Young, Gifted and Black: Lorraine Hansberry in Her Own Words**, adapted by Robert Nemiroff, © 1969. Reprinted by permission of Prentice-Hall, Inc., Englewood Cliffs, NJ

p. 18 from **Selected Poems of Langston Hughes** by Langston Hughes, © 1959. Reprinted by permission of Alfred A. Knopf, Inc., New York, NY

p. 19 from **Their Eyes Were Watching God** by Zora Neale Hurston, © 1937, renewed 1965. Reprinted by permission of Harper & Row Publishers Inc., New York, NY

p. 35 from **The Negro in The Making of America** by Benjamin Quarles, © 1964. Reprinted by permission of Macmillan Publishing Co., New York, NY

p. 47 from **The Poems of Phillis Wheatley**, edited by Julian D. Mason, Jr., © 1966. The University of North Carolina Press. reprinted by permission.

p. 49 from **To Be Equal** by Whitney Young, © 1964. Reprinted by permission of McGraw-Hill Co., New York, NY

Wade Hudson is a playwright, poet, and freelance writer whose published works for children include the books **Pass It On** and **Jamal's Busy Day**, and the play **Freedom Star**. He attended Southern University in Louisiana and the Television and Film School at WNET-Channel 13 in New York City. **Sam Carter Belongs Here**, **The Return**, and **A House Divided** are among the plays written by Mr. Hudson that have been performed on stage. A former public relations specialist, he and his wife, Cheryl, founded Just Us Books, a publishing company that specializes in books for children that focus on the African-American experience, in 1988.

Valerie Wilson Wesley is currently the executive editor of **Essence** magazine. She is co-author of **Book of Black Heroes: Vol. II, Great Women in the Struggle**, published by Just Us Books, and the young-adult novel **Where Do I Go From Here?** (Scholastic, Fall 1993). Her fiction and nonfiction for both adults and children have appeared in numerous publications, including **Essence**, **Ms**, **The New York Times**, and **Scholastic News**. Valerie is the wife of screenwriter-playwright Richard Wesley, and the mother of two college-age daughters.

Cheryl Willis Hudson is an author and graphic designer. She has designed books for Macmillan as well as other major publishing houses. Her stories and illustrations for children have appeared in **Ebony, Jr!** and **Wee Wisdom Magazine**. She is the author of the **AFRO-BETS ABC Book** and the **AFRO-BETS 123 Book**. Ms. Hudson, a native of Portsmouth, Virginia, graduated from Oberlin College in Ohio. She now makes her home in New Jersey with her husband, Wade, and two children, Katura and Stephan.

P. Mignon Hinds is a writer, editor, public relations consultant, and the founder of Mignon Creations & Communications in New York City. She is the author of six children's books and has written for **Essence**, **Black Enterprise** and **Creative Classroom** magazines, as well as numerous corporate publications. Ms. Hinds is a graduate of Hampton University and the City University of New York Graduate School of Education.